Children of the Westward Trail

CHILDREN OF THE WESTWARD TRAIL

R E B E C C A   S T E F O F F

THE MILLBROOK PRESS
BROOKFIELD • CONNECTICUT

Cover photograph courtesy National Museum of American Art,
Washington, D.C./Art Resource, NY

Photographs courtesy of North Wind Picture Archives: pp. 9, 21, 32, 42, 67, 70;
The Bettmann Archive: pp. 13, 19, 27, 36, 46, 55, 59, 62, 78; Western History
Department, Denver Public Library: p. 24; The New York Public Library: p. 31;
National Archives: p. 40; New York Public Library, Picture Collection: pp. 49, 74,
79; Howard Warp Pioneer Village Foundation: p. 52; Oregon Historical Society:
pp. 85 (neg. no. 798), 89 (neg. no. 838); Lee Moorhouse Collection, M534, Special
Collections, University of Oregon Library: p. 87. Map by Frank Senyk.

Library of Congress Cataloging-in-Publication Data
Stefoff, Rebecca, 1951–
Children of the westward trail / by Rebecca Stefoff.
p. cm.
Includes bibliographical references and index.
Summary: Describes what life was like for those children who
were uprooted from their midwestern homes and transported by
their families across the frontier in wagons and on horseback.
ISBN 1-56294-582-3 (lib. bdg.)
1. Pioneer children—West (U.S.)—Juvenile literature. 2. Frontier
and pioneer life—West (U.S.)—Juvenile literature. 3. West (U.S.)
—History—Juvenile literature. [1. Pioneers. 2. Frontier and
pioneer life—West (U.S.) 3. West (U.S.)—History.] I. Title.
F596.S827 1995 917.804′2′083—dc20 95–31040 CIP AC

Contents

Going West

The East Coast of North America was settled by people from Great Britain and other parts of Europe who dreamed of owning land in the New World. As the eastern colonies filled up, land-hungry pioneers kept moving west into new territory, pushing the frontier of settlement westward as they went. By 1800, the frontier had reached the Mississippi River, and Americans began looking across the river toward the plains, mountains, deserts, and fertile valleys of the West.

At first, the West was closed to American settlement because the territory beyond the Mississippi had been claimed by France, Spain, and England. But in 1803, President Thomas Jefferson bought France's claim in a transaction known as the Louisiana Purchase. It was one of history's biggest real estate deals: Jefferson more than doubled the size of the United States, adding present-day Louisiana, Missouri, Arkansas, Iowa, South Dakota, North Dakota, Nebraska, and Oklahoma, along with parts of Kansas, Wyoming, Colorado, Montana, and Minnesota. The Louisiana

Purchase opened the way for Americans to move into the West. The first step, though, was for them to explore their new territory.

From 1804 to 1806, two army officers named Meriwether Lewis and William Clark led an expedition from the Mississippi River all the way to the Pacific Ocean and back again, proving that travelers could cross the western part of the continent. Lewis and Clark—and other explorers who followed them into the West—brought back stories about the rich soil, towering trees, and mild climate of California and Oregon. These stories inspired thousands of settlers to seek new homes in the western territories. Full of hope and determination, the settlers headed toward the sunset on the long, hazardous trail.

Settlers who crossed the Mississippi called themselves "emigrants," which means "people who leave the countries where they were born." These pioneers really were leaving their own country, heading into territory that was not yet part of the United States. Some of the emigrants came from Boston, New York, Philadelphia, and the other crowded, fast-growing cities of the East Coast. Others came from the hills of New York State and New England, the farmlands of the Ohio Valley, and the rural villages of the South. All of them turned their backs on the familiar landscapes of home. They set their faces toward the strange and beckoning lands of the West—toward the Great Plains, the Rocky Mountains, and a new home at journey's end.

Just like the colonists who had crossed the Atlantic

Travelers ride carefully down the steep Sierra Nevada range into California's Yosemite Valley. After hearing the stories told by explorers and fur trappers, many Easterners were eager to see the grand, wild landscapes of the West.

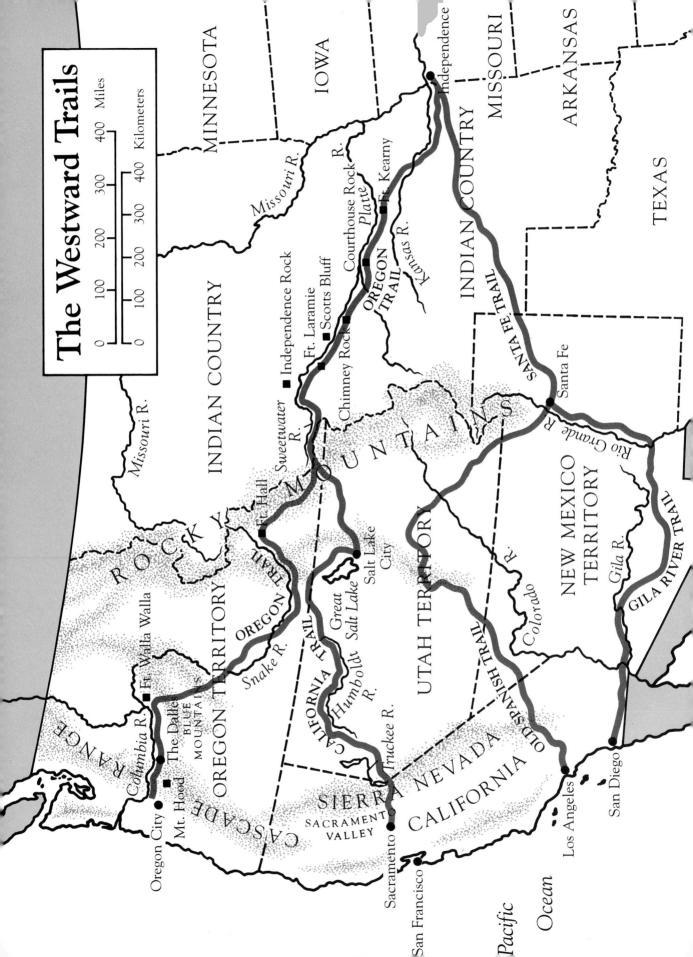

The Westward Trails

400 Miles

400 Kilometers

0 100 200 300 400
0 100 200 300 400

MINNESOTA

IOWA

Independence

MISSOURI

ARKANSAS

TEXAS

INDIAN COUNTRY

Missouri R.

Ft. Kearny

Platte R.

Courthouse Rock

Scotts Bluff

Chimney Rock

Ft. Laramie

Independence Rock

OREGON TRAIL

Kansas R.

INDIAN COUNTRY

SANTA FE TRAIL

Santa Fe

Rio Grande R.

Sweetwater R.

Missouri R.

INDIAN COUNTRY

R O C K Y   M O U N T A I N S

Ft. Hall

OREGON TRAIL

Snake R.

OREGON TERRITORY

Ft. Walla Walla

BLUE MOUNTAINS

The Dalles

Columbia R.

Mt. Hood

Oregon City

CASCADE RANGE

CALIFORNIA TRAIL

Great Salt Lake

Salt Lake City

Humboldt R.

Truckee R.

UTAH TERRITORY

Colorado R.

NEW MEXICO TERRITORY

Gila R.

GILA RIVER TRAIL

OLD SPANISH TRAIL

SIERRA NEVADA

SACRAMENTO VALLEY

Sacramento

San Francisco

CALIFORNIA

Los Angeles

San Diego

Pacific Ocean

Ocean to settle on the East Coast of America, the emigrants who crossed the continent to settle on the West Coast wanted to build a better life for themselves and their families. People from crowded areas, or from places where the soil was losing its fertility because of overfarming, hoped to own bigger and better farms in the western territories. Craftspeople and merchants believed that their wares would bring good prices in the new settlements out West. And, after gold was discovered in California in 1848, many emigrants hoped to strike it rich in the gold fields.

Some of the emigrants were drawn west by the pure love of adventure. These hardy souls felt that the eastern part of the country was becoming too "civilized," too full of rules and laws and tidy neighborhoods, and they longed for the wide-open spaces of the West. One Illinois farmer explained that he had to move on because people were settling "right under his nose"—even though his closest neighbor was 12 miles (19 kilometers) away. He took his family to Missouri, but before he had finished clearing a place to build a cabin he decided that Missouri was just as crowded as Illinois. Finally he went all the way to the Oregon Territory and built a home on the shore of the Pacific Ocean, with only the waves and the seagulls for neighbors.

It did not take long for explorers, soldiers, missionaries, and settlers to tame the American West. Most of the earliest settlements were on the West Coast, which could be reached by sea as well as by land. The goal of many of the first emigrants was the Oregon Territory that Lewis and

Clark had described in such glowing terms. Americans who went to California usually settled in communities that had been established years earlier by the Spanish. Then, beginning in the 1840s, settlements sprouted up around the military forts and trading posts along the emigrant trails. Outposts such as Fort Hall in Idaho were the starting points for communities in the Rocky Mountain states. The last part of the West to be settled was the Great Plains. This vast sweep of land between the Mississippi and the Rocky Mountains had been set aside as Indian Territory, but by the 1870s the Native American peoples had been removed to reservations, and settlers were moving onto the plains.

In 1869, just sixty-three years after Lewis and Clark returned from their historic journey, the first railroad across the country was completed. Where Lewis and Clark and their followers had trudged for week after weary week, crossing endless plains and inching their way up steep mountain passes, the roaring, soot-belching locomotives carried travelers in a few days. By the time the railroad was finished, Texas, Wisconsin, California, Minnesota, Oregon, Kansas, Nevada, and Nebraska had become states. By the end of the 1890s, Colorado, Washington, North and South Dakota, Montana, Wyoming, Idaho, and Utah were also states. The United States stretched from sea to sea. The frontier had vanished. Yet stories of the frontier continued to fascinate people. Historians today say that the settling of the West was one of the most important chapters in American history. It was certainly one of the most colorful.

A young emigrant offers two grouse, his contribution to the evening meal. Nearby, younger children examine a deer that has been shot. Emigration was a family affair, and many families had half a dozen or more children.

Between 1806 and 1900, more than half a million men, women, and children followed the westward trails. Most people went west in family groups, and perhaps as many as half of all the emigrants were children. These children saw the westward trail from their own point of view. Although their parents may have regarded the journey as a difficult ordeal, many emigrant children saw it as fun. To some children, the crossing of the continent seemed like a great, lighthearted adventure—an outdoor game or camping trip on a huge scale. Other children, though, saw a darker side of the westward trail. Some encountered fear, hunger, loneliness, and death.

Quite a few of the young people who traveled west in the nineteenth century knew that they were making history, taking part in a large movement that would change the shape of the United States. They kept diaries or wrote letters to friends and relatives back home, telling of the sights they saw and the events they experienced. Sometimes, years later, after they were grown up, people who had come west as children wrote or talked about their adventures in "the old days."

A few children's accounts of the westward journey were published in magazines or books. Many others lay hidden and forgotten in dusty attics for years. Today, historical societies across the country are working to find and preserve these priceless messages from the past. These old documents are pieces of history, for history does not belong only to famous people, such as kings and presidents and inventors. History is also told in the voices of ordinary people — including children.

One child who made the journey west was Martha Gay of Missouri, who traveled to the Oregon Territory when she was thirteen years old. Many years later, she wrote the story of her childhood and the journey west so that the children of later generations would know what it was like to be a child crossing the country in a wagon train. In the chapters that follow, we will learn about Martha's experiences, and we will see that thousands of other young Americans shared those experiences. They knew what it was like to say good-bye to their homes and their friends, and to live for months in strange and uncomfortable surroundings. They knew the pain of losing a loved one to the dangers of the trail; they shared the excitement of greeting a baby sister or brother born along the way. They were the boys and girls who helped to settle the American West—the children of the westward trail.

Chapter One

Leavetaking

As far as Martha Gay was concerned, Missouri was the perfect place to grow up. When Martha was a little girl, her family lived on a farm. With her brothers, Martha rambled through the forest, feasting on wild plums and grapes and gathering strawberries and wildflowers. She called herself a tomboy: an adventurous girl who was brave enough to explore dark, cold caves with her big brothers.

Country life was full of excitement and danger, such as the time a large wolf followed Martha's older sister, Mamie, home from school. Martha's father killed the wolf and gave its cubs to Mamie as pets. The Gay children also made pets of the farm's lambs, ducks, and chickens. They learned to ride horses, to milk cows, and to fish and hunt.

When Martha was nine years old, the Gay family left the farm and moved into town. The year was 1846, and the town was Springfield, Missouri. Martha's father worked as a carpenter, while her mother was busy taking care of the house and the children. Martha missed the farm. "I did not like our town home very well at first," she recalled many years later, "but when I got acquainted with some children and accustomed to the place, I became very fond of life there. Mother was well pleased. We soon had friends about us and were happy in our new home." Before long Martha had made friends with some of the girls in the local school. She and her sister often spent the night at the home of one friend or another. Martha felt right at home in Springfield and expected that she would live there for the rest of her life.

Everything changed one day in 1850, when Martha's father came down with what she called "the Western fever." Ever since the early 1840s, emigrants had been gathering along the Mississippi and Missouri rivers. Each spring, huge wagon trains of settlers headed westward, bound for new territories. Many Missouri towns were "jumping-off places" for the wagon trains. In the jumping-off places, townsfolk like Martha's father watched the settlers depart year after year and listened to their excited talk about the wonderful new land that waited at the end of the trail. Sometimes the townsfolk got caught up in the excitement and decided that they, too, should head west.

Martha's father had a good reason for wanting to take his family to the Oregon Territory. There were nine boys in the Gay family, and each of these boys would want to own his own land one day. But land was getting expensive in Missouri. Mr. Gay knew that it would be a struggle for all of his sons to buy farms or homesteads when they grew up. In the

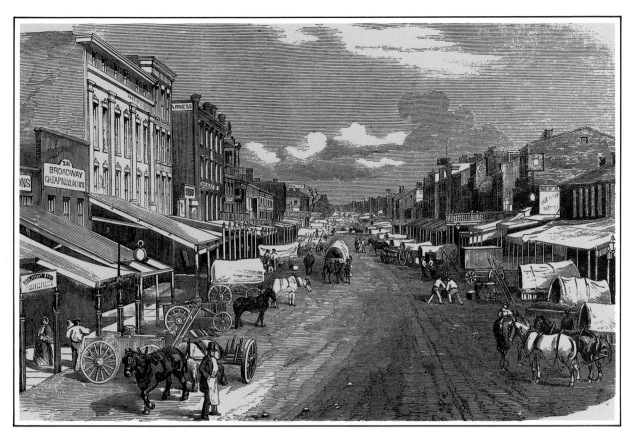

Shops in St. Louis did a brisk business in the 1850s. St. Louis and other Missouri towns were "jumping-off places" for emigrants heading West. This drawing shows emigrants outfitting their wagons with supplies for the trip.

Oregon Territory, however, land was free. It belonged to anyone who settled on it and used it. In Oregon, each of Martha's brothers could eventually claim a farm or homestead of his own.

Free land was a powerful attraction, but the idea of emigrating did not sound good to everyone. When Mr. Gay told his family that they would be going west to Oregon, Mrs. Gay and the eleven children were dismayed.

"Mother was not willing to go," said Martha. "She did

not want to undertake the long and dangerous journey with a large family of small children. To cross the plains in those days with ox teams was a fearful undertaking and a tiresome one too. She begged father to give up the notion but he could not." Martha's father could not get Oregon out of his head. He received a letter from an old neighbor who had gone west several years earlier. In this letter, the neighbor talked about the lovely land, gentle climate, and rich mines of the West. Mr. Gay read the letter over and over again, and each reading made him more determined than ever to emigrate.

Finally, reluctantly, Martha's mother agreed to go. The next step for Martha's father was to tell the children of his plans. "He said he wanted us all to go with him to the new country," Martha wrote later. "He told us about the great Pacific Ocean, the Columbia River, and beautiful Willamette Valley, the great forests and the snowcapped mountains. He then explained the hardships and dangers, the sufferings and the dreary long days we would journey on and on before we would reach Oregon."

After he had told the children all about the Oregon Territory and the journey they would have to make to get there, Mr. Gay asked the children if they wanted to make the trip. Martha and her brothers and sisters did not think much of the idea. They told their father that they would rather stay in Springfield with their friends. "But children were expected to do as their parents said in those days," Martha wrote, "and father said we must come." In truth, the chil-

An early picture of the Oregon Territory shows the Columbia River and Mount St. Helens in the distance. After Martha Gay's father caught the "Oregon fever," he tried to get the children excited about Oregon by telling them they would see "great forests and snowcapped mountains."

dren had no say in the matter, and even Martha's mother could do little to change her husband's mind.

Most of the women who made the westward journey did so only because their husbands, fathers, or brothers insisted on it. The women—and quite a few of the children—would have been happier staying at home. Some families had already moved once, twice, or even more often, coming from New England or the Carolinas to Kentucky, Illinois, or Missouri in their search for the perfect place in which to settle down. Before deciding to go to Oregon, for example, Mr. Gay had moved his family from Kentucky to Tennessee, then to Missouri, then to Arkansas (where Martha was born), and finally back to Missouri. Mrs. Gay and the children were tired of packing up and moving every few years. They had had a chance to put down roots in Springfield, to form friendships, and to feel at home. It was not surprising that they wanted to stay there. But in those days the husband and father was the head of the family, and everyone obeyed his wishes. In 1850 a pioneer woman named Margaret Wilson wrote a letter to her mother, breaking the sad news that her husband had decided to emigrate to California. "I am going with him," wrote Mrs. Wilson, "as there is no alternative."

Mrs. Gay and her children were not the only ones who tried to talk Mr. Gay out of going west. Martha wrote, "Friends and relatives who had heard of our intended journey came from far and near to persuade father to give up the wild notion. They said the family would be slain by Indians or perish on the deserts. But father had made up his mind."

Martha Gay's father was just one of thousands of men who caught "the Western fever." One child remembered hearing a man named Mr. Burnett talk about the wonders of the Oregon Territory: "Mr. Burnett hauled a box out onto the sidewalk, took his stand upon it, and began to tell us about the land flowing with milk and honey upon the shores of the Pacific." Mr. Burnett described great crops of wheat, rich soil, and mild weather. The child's father was so excited by what he heard that he decided then and there to go to Oregon. He was the first to sign up to join a wagon train bound for the West.

A pioneer woman told how she and her family happened to emigrate. In the winter of 1846, one of her neighbors got hold of a book about California. "He began talking of moving to the new country," the woman said, "and he brought the book to my husband to read, and he was carried away with the idea too. I said, 'Oh, let us not go.'" But the woman's protests made no difference. In the end, she and her husband sold their home, and then they sold or gave away all of their possessions that they could not take with them. They set out for California with nothing but a wagon full of household goods, a map of the trail, and high hopes.

Family members may have disagreed about whether or not they should go west, but once the decision had been made, families were united. Large families turned to one another for support. Often grandparents, aunts and uncles, and cousins emigrated together. People knew that the trip west would demand all of their strength, and that getting started in a new part of the country would also be difficult. They knew that they could rely on their relatives if they needed help. Parents were especially worried about what might happen to children whose mothers and fathers died on the journey. People who traveled with cousins, in-laws, or other relatives knew that there would always be kinfolk on hand to take care of orphans.

An emigrant family poses for a photographic record of their journey—perhaps the only photograph that would ever be taken of them. Such pictures were precious keepsakes for family members who were separated from their loved ones.

Sometimes older people decided to go west with their children and grandchildren, fearing that if they stayed behind they would never see their loved ones again. When the James Reed family set out from Illinois for California in 1846, for example, they were accompanied by Mrs. Reed's elderly mother, Sarah Keyes. Although Mrs. Keyes was in poor health and not well suited for the challenge of a long trip over rough country, she refused to be parted from her daughter and grandchildren. Another elderly emigrant was Tabitha Brown, who was sixty-six years old when she went to Oregon in 1846 with two of her married children and their families.

Sadly, however, many of the children who took the westward trail had to say farewell to their grandparents and to other loved ones who were not making the trip. Although some emigrants traveled with large groups of kinfolk, other clans were split up by emigration.

Martha Gay's family was almost divided on the eve of departure. Martha's oldest brother, James, had married just a few months earlier, and his young bride, Frances, had promised to go west with him and the rest of the Gays. As the time of departure grew near, Frances's parents and kin told her not to go. They said that if she remained in Missouri, James would be certain to stay behind also. "But when they saw James take his whip and start his team out," said Martha, "they gave up the idea." Frances's father, brother, and sister brought her to James, pleading with the Gays to look after Frances and protect her from danger.

"The saddest parting of all," Martha wrote, "was when my mother took leave of her aged and sorrowing mother, knowing full well they would never meet again on earth." The western settlements were so far away that most people made the journey only once. Letters could travel back and forth, slowly and uncertainly, but people rarely did. Martha kissed her grandmother good-bye knowing that she would never see her again.

Leavetakings were big events. Friends, relatives, and neighbors gathered to bid farewell to the emigrants. Lillie Marcks, who was seven years old when her family took her west from Ohio in 1869, long remembered the way her family's friends crowded around them at the parting. "Some cried and talked of Indians and bears," she said.

When the Reed family left Illinois, the whole town turned out to see them off. "My father with tears in his eyes tried to smile as one friend after another grasped his hand in a last farewell," Virginia Reed wrote later. "Mama was overcome with grief. At last we were all in the wagons, the drivers cracked their whips, the oxen moved slowly forward, and the long journey had begun." Virginia and her two younger sisters and younger brother kissed their friends good-bye and climbed onto the high seat of their wagon. Turning in their seats, they waved until their friends and their old home were lost to sight.

The Gay family's send-off from Springfield was a holiday for the whole community. Stores and schools were closed so that people could say good-bye to the emigrants. "The house and yard and streets were crowded with people," said Martha. "Friends and schoolmates were crying all around us." People made speeches wishing the Gays health and good fortune in their new home. Finally, the moment of departure arrived. "We took a long last look at all," Martha wrote, "then closed our eyes on the scene and moved forward." The sound of crying echoed in Martha's ears as the wagon rolled away.

Many children smiled and laughed as they set out on the long pioneer road. The journey seemed like a glorious adventure, and the children expected to have fun all the way.

Not all departures were tearful. Sad though they were to be leaving their homes, friends, and grandparents, many of the emigrant children were thrilled at the thought of what lay ahead. As they gazed at the westward trail unrolling in front of them all the way to the far horizon, they looked forward to new sights, new friends, and new adventures. Fifteen-year-old Rebecca Nutting was excited on the day her family left Iowa in 1850, headed for the California gold fields. "Oh, we were going to have just a happy time," she wrote in her diary.

Chapter Two

Home on the Road

Emigrants who took the westward trail spent a long time getting ready for the trip. For Martha Gay and her family, the preparations took more than a year. Martha and her brothers and sister had plenty of time to get used to the idea of going west and to visit all of their friends.

One important part of the preparations was selling the family's property in Missouri—both the house in Springfield and the farm in the country. As soon as he decided to emigrate, Mr. Gay started looking for someone to buy his property. He also had to close up his carpentry business. This meant finishing work he had promised to do, collecting money that was owed to him, and paying his debts.

Many of the emigrants were unable to get a good price for their property. If people knew that a man was in a hurry to sell up and move west, they would try to buy his property cheaply. If he needed to sell badly enough, he might accept a low price. Some emigrants could not sell their land and houses at all; they simply left their homes standing empty.

While Martha's father was arranging the sale of the family property, he was also getting together the things that the family would take on the journey west. The Gay party would be a large one. In addition to Mr. and Mrs. Gay, their nine sons and two daughters, and their son James's wife, the party would include several hired men. Single men who wanted to go west generally joined a family party. The men helped with the work of handling the wagons and the livestock; in return, the women of the party cooked their meals and did their laundry.

Getting any family ready for the westward trail was a big job, but outfitting a group as large as the Gay party was a huge task. Fortunately, the emigrants could find plenty of advice about what to take and how to prepare. Soon after the first big group of emigrants went west in 1841, emigrant handbooks began to be published in the East. These books contained descriptions of the westward routes and lists of necessary supplies. People who were planning to emigrate also received useful tips from friends and relatives who had gone west before them and who wrote home with advice.

Everyone agreed that the most important piece of equipment for the trip was the wagon. Nearly all of the nineteenth-century emigrants crossed the country in wagon trains. They did not ride in the tall Conestoga wagons that are sometimes seen in movies or television shows about the Old West. The Conestoga wagons were designed by Penn-

One of the first and most popular guidebooks for emigrants was written by Lansford W. Hastings. Some of his advice, however, was dangerous. Hastings told the Donner Party to take a "cut-off," but his shortcut led the emigrants into disaster.

THE

EMIGRANTS' GUIDE,

TO

OREGON AND CALIFORNIA,

CONTAINING SCENES AND INCIDENTS OF A PARTY OF
OREGON EMIGRANTS;

A DESCRIPTION OF OREGON;

SCENES AND INCIDENTS OF A PARTY OF CALIFORNIA
EMIGRANTS;

AND

A DESCRIPTION OF CALIFORNIA;

WITH

A DESCRIPTION OF THE DIFFERENT ROUTES TO
THOSE COUNTRIES

AND

ALL NECESSARY INFORMATION RELATIVE TO THE
EQUIPMENT, SUPPLIES, AND THE METHOD
OF TRAVELING.

BY LANSFORD W. HASTINGS,
Leader of the Oregon and California Emigrants of 1842.

CINCINNATI:
PUBLISHED BY GEORGE CONCLIN,
STEREOTYPED BY SHEPARD & CO.
- 1845.

sylvania Dutch craftsmen in the eighteenth century. The fronts and backs of their large canopies were tall and slanted, with a curved silhouette like that of a boat. These immense wagons were used to haul large loads on freight

A sturdy wagon and a team of strong oxen were the most important parts of the emigrant's equipment. The wagon pictured here has a rocking chair, a trunk, and a chicken coop tied on behind. A barrel—perhaps containing tar or grease—is fastened to the underside of the wagon.

trails in the eastern part of the country. They were too big and too heavy for the rough, narrow mountain passages of the westward trails.

The wagon used by the emigrants was shaped like an ordinary farm wagon, with a flat bed about 6 feet wide and 10 or 12 feet long (2 by 3 or 3.5 meters). The sides were 2 or 3 feet (.5 to 1 meter) high. Because the emigrants would have to cross many rivers and streams, the wagons were designed to be used as boats when necessary. Tar buckets hung from the sides of the wagons; when the emigrants came to a river crossing, they filled the cracks between the boards with tar to make the wagons waterproof.

Wooden hoops were raised above the wagon bed to support the roof canopy, which was a double layer of canvas. Usually the canopy was oiled to help keep out the rain. The outside of each wagon was festooned with gear: water barrels that would be refilled by every rainstorm or at every stream; buckets of grease to keep the wheels turning smoothly; spare wooden wheels and axles to replace those that would break along the way; coils of heavy rope for lowering the wagons down steep hills; and extra leather harnesses for the animals that would pull the wagon.

Every emigrant knew that the family's comfort—perhaps even its survival—depended upon a sturdy, well-built wagon that could carry about 2,500 pounds (1,134 kilograms) of cargo. Martha Gay's father ordered his four wagons from a wagon-builder, but some emigrants could not afford to buy wagons. They had to build them. A boy named Benjamin

Bonney and his father worked for months to make their emigrant wagon.

A few of the wealthier emigrants traveled in luxury in specially equipped wagons. The Reed family of Illinois started west in a fancy two-story wagon that had a stove and built-in beds. Young Virginia Reed called it their "pioneer palace car." People came from far around to marvel at the Reeds' huge wagon as they set off on their journey.

The emigrant wagons were pulled by oxen. Fully loaded, a typical wagon required eight to twelve oxen, yoked together in pairs, to move it. The wagons could also be pulled by horses or mules, but experience had taught the emigrants that oxen were the best choice. Horses were faster, but they tired more quickly and were not strong enough to haul heavy wagons up steep slopes. Mules were strong but ornery. Their stubbornness made them difficult to handle. Oxen, however, plodded patiently along day after day, pulling huge loads. Yet even these big, strong beasts sometimes dropped in their tracks during the journey west, exhausted by overwork or weakened by shortages of food and water. Wise travelers had extra oxen tied to the back of the wagon.

A suitable wagon and a team of oxen cost between $400 and $600. This was an emigrant's biggest expense. Yet there were many other expenses involved in fitting out a family for the westward trail. The emigrants had to carry with them not only everything they needed for the journey but also everything they would need to get started in their new western homes. Those who planned to start farms had to carry seeds, plows, and tools; those who planned to open businesses had to carry merchandise or equipment. Clara Brown, an African-American woman who emigrated from Missouri to Denver, Colorado, in 1859, was a launderer who needed to take her big washtubs west so that she could earn her living when she arrived in Denver. She persuaded the master of a wagon train to carry both her and her washtubs in exchange for doing the emigrants' laundry along the way.

In 1864, Pamelia Fergus of Minnesota was getting ready to take her four children west to join their father, who was prospecting a gold claim in Montana. She received a letter from her husband containing a long list of things she should pack. The list was divided into sections such as Provisions, Clothing, Extras for Use on the Road, and so on. Under the heading Provisions, Mr. Fergus had listed the food Mrs. Fergus should buy for the trip: 600 pounds (272 kilograms) of flour, 400 (181) of sugar, 300 (136) of cornmeal, 100 (45) of rice, and 50 pounds (23 kilograms) each of beans, cheese, and butter. She should also have two barrels of crackers, 20 gallons (76 liters) of maple syrup, and supplies of tea, coffee, salt, bacon, ham, salted codfish, and dried beef, fruits, and vegetables. On the trail Mrs. Fergus would prepare her family's meals using a small camp stove, one or two kettles, and several frying pans. But she also had to carry everything she would need to set up a kitchen in her new Montana home. Her kitchen equipment included a large cookstove, bread pans, milk cans, water buckets, and dishes.

Pamelia Fergus's provisions were more varied and more

Emigrant women faced the challenge of feeding their hungry families on the road. This woman is lucky—she has a portable camp stove. Some women had to cook over open fires of wood or buffalo dung.

generous than those of the average emigrant. One of the most popular emigrant handbooks said that a traveler on the western trail could get by with 200 pounds (90 kilograms) of flour, 150 pounds (68 kilograms) of bacon, 20 pounds (9 kilograms) of sugar, and 10 pounds (4.5 kilograms) each of coffee and salt. Even without costly spices and special treats, provisions for the journey could cost a family $300 to $600. Martha Gay's family was larger than average. The provisions they assembled for the journey were "enough to stock a small grocery store," Martha said.

Rifles and ammunition might add another $100 or so to the cost of outfitting a family for the journey, but no emigrant would have set foot on the westward trail without them. The guns would be used for hunting game along the way and also, if necessary, for defense. Martha Gay's father equipped the men and boys in his party not just with rifles but also with pistols. Decked out in their gunbelts, Martha's older brothers looked to her like "land pirates."

Clothing was another very important part of a family's equipment. Travelers needed well-made, sturdy clothes that would stand up to the hard treatment they would receive on the trail. Women and girls usually had two or three dresses, as well as shawls, aprons, and nightgowns. Men and boys needed two or three pairs of pants and half a dozen heavy woolen shirts. Emigrant women kept their sewing kits close at hand for repairs on the trail. Everyone had to have several pairs of strong boots or shoes; there was no chance to buy new boots along the way, although some travelers did try wearing Indian moccasins and found them to be quite comfortable.

Most clothing in those days was hand-sewn. Martha Gay helped make the clothes for her thirteen-member family's journey. "Dozens of garments of all sizes and all colors were in progress," she said. "For more than a year the sewing was done, all by hand. Many neighbors came to the sewing bees. How they would talk and cry over their sewing, saying we would all surely be lost crossing the plains."

The basic cost of equipping a family for the journey west was $500 to $1,000, depending upon the size of the family and how much of the necessary equipment they already owned. Some families spent much more; others scraped by on almost nothing, traveling with scanty provisions and cheap, patched-up gear. Most scrimped and saved to prepare for the journey, which was considered a very costly venture. One family with seven children saved money for four years to pay for the trip, and even then they had to borrow $500 from a relative.

The western territories were not completely out of touch with the rest of the world. Ships from many countries landed regularly in harbors from California to Canada, and goods of various sorts could be purchased in the settlements there. Still, some things were hard to find or very expensive on the West Coast. As the emigrants stocked their wagons, therefore, they stowed away many small, important items that would be useful but difficult to obtain in their new homes. These included needles, writing paper and pens, medicines, books, lanterns, and matches. Many emigrants carried Bibles. After photography became common, they also carried pictures of the loved ones they had left behind.

Children looked forward to the long trip and the new territory as a permanent holiday from school. Yet many pioneer parents were determined that their children would get an education. Sometimes even parents who could barely read and write themselves carried a few books and pencils and a writing slate so that their sons and daughters would have *some* learning materials in their new home. A few children of the westward trail even did schoolwork during the journey. Barsina Rogers French, who crossed the southern desert to the Arizona Territory in 1867 at the age of thirteen, studied grammar and practiced her writing along the way.

Sacrifices were part of emigration. Not only did people have to leave behind their homes and loved ones, but they often had to give up cherished possessions as well. Most emigrant wagons could not hold large pieces of furniture—even furniture that had been passed down from earlier generations. Such items had to be sold or given away. Precious china plates and teacups had to be exchanged for unbreakable tin ones. Sometimes even heirloom quilts that had been lovingly made by an emigrant's mother or grandmother had to be left behind. Pamelia Fergus's husband warned her not to bring her quilts on the westward trail because they tore too easily. He told her to replace the quilts with tough woolen blankets.

Some emigrants did try to carry their best-loved possessions with them. It seemed that it would be easy enough to carry a chest of drawers, a bedstead, or a rocking chair across the continent—and, after all, the emigrants would need furniture once they were settled in the new territories. But

An emigrant wagon is ready for the journey, crammed with precious items. In addition to clothing, a bureau, and a chair, it carries a spinning wheel and a butter churn (on the right side).

more often than not, the furniture never reached the west. Somewhere along the way—perhaps when the oxen grew too weary to pull the heavy load, or when the wagon had to be stripped of its contents for the haul up a steep hill—the chest of drawers or the rocking chair would be abandoned. The most rugged parts of the trail were lined with the belongings of emigrants who had been desperate to lighten their loads. Abandoned furniture cracked in the heat and rotted in the rain beside dusty piles of dishes and trunks full of books.

One boy who came west with his family when he was five years old later remembered how his mother had held him on her lap and cried as their wagon rolled away from her dearest possession, a mahogany sideboard that had belonged to her grandmother. Lucy Ann Henderson, who was eleven when her family took the westward trail, recalled that the men of the wagon train held a meeting and decided to throw away every bit of surplus weight so that the wagons could move faster. "A man named Smith had a wooden rolling pin that it was decided was useless and must be abandoned," Lucy said. "I shall never forget how that big man stood there with tears streaming down his face as he said, 'Do I have to throw this away? It was my mother's. I remember she always used it to roll out her biscuits, and they were awful good biscuits.' "

Some emigrants did manage to save their treasured possessions, even in the most dreadful circumstances. One of the most famous of all the items carried west by the emigrants is a little doll that belonged to Patty Reed, Virginia Reed's eight-year-old sister. The Reeds were part of a wagon train that was called the Donner Party because it was led by a man named George Donner. The Donner Party's journey to California was the worst disaster in the history of the westward migration. Half of the people in the wagon train died, and the survivors lost their wagons, their livestock, and almost everything else they possessed. After terrible suffering,

When oxen collapsed or died, emigrants were in a desperate situation. Some had to leave their most beloved possessions behind in the hope of making it to the end of the trail with a lighter load.

they finished the journey by crossing the rugged Sierra Nevada mountain range on foot in deep snow. Patty Reed was one of the survivors. At journey's end, she reached into her clothing and pulled out her doll. She had carried it, hidden under her clothes, for many long and weary miles, afraid that if the grown-ups saw it, they would make her throw it away to lighten the load.

Chapter Three

Choosing
a Route

When emigration to the western territories began in the middle of the nineteenth century, there were two main routes across the continent. Both of them started in the jumping-off communities near the Mississippi and Missouri rivers. Some emigrants began their journeys from Nauvoo, Illinois; from St. Joseph or Liberty, Missouri; or from Council Bluffs, Iowa, but most started from Independence, Missouri, on the banks of the Missouri River. Independence is generally considered to be the beginning of the two main westward routes, the Santa Fe Trail and the Oregon Trail.

The Santa Fe Trail, the older of the two, was opened in 1821. At first it was a trade route along which traders and their goods traveled back and forth between Missouri and the Spanish settlement at Santa Fe, New Mexico. After Texas, Arizona, and New Mexico became United States territories in the 1840s, the Santa Fe Trail became the settlers' highway into the arid southwest. It led west across the southern part of what is now Kansas to an outpost called Bent's Fort in Colorado. From there it dipped sharply south toward Santa Fe.

Travelers who wanted to go farther west could take the Old Spanish Trail, which had been used for several centuries by Spanish explorers, missionaries, and traders who criss-crossed the Southwest. This trail led through some extremely rugged country in present-day southern Utah—a region of steep, twisting canyons, jagged mountains, and dry plateaus—before crossing southern California to reach the ocean at Los Angeles.

Most of the emigrants bound for the western territories used the Oregon Trail, which was also called the Oregon and California Trail, the Great Overland Trail, the Emigrant Road, the Platte Road, and the Oregon Trace. Whatever name was used, this was the route that carried hundreds of thousands of settlers to California and to the Oregon Territory (which included Idaho and Washington and parts of Montana and Wyoming, as well as the present-day state of Oregon).

The Oregon Trail was opened in 1841 by a small group of emigrants—thirty-five men, five women, and ten children—who started west from Independence in May. They had no map and no compass. One of the men claimed to have seen a map in a book; perhaps this was the map of the American West that William Clark drew after the return of the Lewis and Clark Expedition.

The emigrants were bound for Oregon, but they could not take the northerly route along the Missouri River that Lewis and Clark had taken. The powerful Blackfoot Confederation, a group of Native American tribes who were opposed to white settlement in their lands, blocked that route from the 1820s through the 1840s. Instead, the emigrants planned to follow a route to Oregon that had been taken by a few explorers, soldiers, and traders in the 1830s. The emigrants figured that if they followed the Platte River west and then just kept heading toward the setting sun, they would probably get to where they wanted to go.

After two months, seven of the men turned back to Missouri. The rest of the group pressed on. In early August the emigrants reached Fort Hall, a trading post in what is now southeastern Idaho. Here they split up, with some people heading northwest for Oregon's Willamette Valley and some heading southwest for California. Each group eventually reached its goal. The Oregon Trail had been born.

The following year, about a hundred emigrants took the westward trail. By now, Americans were getting excited about the wonderful territories on the continent's western rim. Rumors flew. People said that the soil in Oregon was so rich that wheat grew taller than a man's head. They said that the land was like paradise, full of berries and honey and every good thing, and that fish leaped out of the river into the fisherman's hand.

In the spring of 1843, the Iowa *Gazette* reported, "The Oregon fever is raging in almost every part of the Union."

An early emigrant group fords the Platte River. Broad, muddy, and winding, the Platte guided the travelers through 450 miles (724 kilometers) of tall grass, prairie, and high plains.

That spring, emigrants from all over the United States gathered in Independence to form wagon trains. More than a thousand people—with 120 wagons and 3,500 head of cattle—went to Oregon in 1843 in what was called the Great Emigration. The numbers continued to rise each year. In the late 1840s and the early 1850s, tens of thousands of people went to Oregon every year, and tens of thousands more went to California.

Many of the children who made the journey had no idea

where they were going or what to expect. Jesse Applegate was seven years old when his family joined the Great Emigration of 1843. One afternoon he asked, "Where are we trying to get to?" Someone answered, "To Oregon." Jesse later wrote, "I think I made up my mind then and there not to ask that question any more. To me, 'Oregon' was a word without meaning."

The Oregon Trail headed west from Independence across the Great Plains. It passed through a corner of what is now the state of Kansas and then angled north into Nebraska. Congress had set aside the Great Plains as Indian Territory, and whites could not settle there, although they could pass through on their way to territories farther west.

Crossing the Great Plains in those days was an extraordinary experience. The tall-grass prairie that stretched for hundred of miles had never known a plow. The prairie grasses sometimes rose higher than a man on horseback; the only way the emigrants could see ahead was to stand on the backs of their horses or oxen. The grass hid the beds of the passing wagons; only their white canopies showed, floating along above the top of the grass. In the early years, before the trail had been worn clear by the passage of hundreds of wagons, emigrants cursed the tough grasses that snared their wagon wheels, and children on foot sometimes got lost in the forest of grass.

Yet travelers also marveled at the beauty of the prairie. In ·spring the grasslands were starred with yellow, white, and blue wildflowers. At this early stage of the journey, when the mood was still light-hearted, the girls of the wagon train would gather wildflowers and weave them into wreaths. Sometimes every ox wore a colorful necklace of flowers.

About 200 miles (322 kilometers) out of Independence, the travelers came to the Platte River, which was to be their constant companion for the next 450 miles (724 kilometers). The Platte was a broad, brown ribbon that stretched away into the west. It was so muddy that some emigrants called it "moving sand." Others complained that it was "too dirty to bathe in, and too thick to drink." In spite of these shortcomings, the Platte was the emigrants' guide west through Nebraska and halfway through what is now Wyoming. Some wagon trains traveled on its north bank, some on its south.

As they rolled along beside the Platte, the emigrants entered the strange new world of the high plains. They saw prairie dog towns; the children laughed with delight at the antics of the plump brown rodents darting in and out of their burrows. The emigrants also saw their first buffalo, moving in vast herds across the prairie. Their passage shook the earth and raised huge clouds of dust. Jesse Applegate recalled that when the cry of "Buffalo!" went up, the men and boys would grab their rifles and rush off to the hunt. That night the emigrants would feast on fresh roasted meat.

The buffalo were useful in another way, too. As the lush tall-grass prairie gave way to the dry short-grass prairie farther west, trees became scarce. With no wood to use as fuel, the emigrants burned dried buffalo dung, which they called

One traveler wrote that the prairie dog towns of the high plains were as big and crowded as the largest cities of Europe. The children had never seen anything like them, for prairie dogs do not live in the eastern states.

"buffalo chips." To the surprise of many pioneer women who were not happy about having to cook their family's meals over burning dung, the chips made good fuel.

Along the Platte the emigrants saw a number of large, unusual rock formations. The most striking of these was Chimney Rock, a broad base from which jutted a tall, narrow spire that could be seen for miles across the plains.

Other rock landmarks included Courthouse Rock and Scotts Bluff, which is now a national monument. On this stretch of the trail the emigrants also came to a few trading posts: Fort Kearny where the trail met the Platte River, Scotts Bluff, and Fort Laramie in Wyoming. Here they could rest themselves and their oxen for a few days and stock up on provisions. They could also leave letters that would be carried back to the States by the next returning trader.

By the time they reached Fort Laramie, the emigrants had traveled about 650 miles (1,046 kilometers) from Independence. Yet they had covered less than one third of the total length of the trail, which was about 2,200 miles (3,500 kilometers) long. Moving on from Fort Laramie, the wagon trains began climbing up into the Rocky Mountains. The summer days were hot, but nights grew colder as the wagons climbed higher.

Thunderstorms were common in the mountains in the summer; the emigrants were soaked by torrential summer rainstorms and pelted by hailstones the size of snowballs. A ten-year-old emigrant girl long remembered a storm that burst over her wagon train in 1846: "The whole sky became black as ink. The rain came down in bucketfuls, drenching us to the skin. There wasn't a tent in camp that held against the terrific wind. The men had to chain the wagons together to keep them from being blown into the river." Young Jesse Applegate's party was overtaken by a surprise snowstorm in the mountains. Said Jesse, "I remember wading through mud and snow and suffering from the cold and wet."

About 900 miles (1,450 kilometers) from Independence, Missouri, the emigrants came to another landmark of the trail: a huge rock formation called Independence Rock. Early explorers and fur trappers had inscribed their names on Independence Rock, and the emigrants continued this practice. Some carved their names into the stone, but most painted them or wrote them in axle grease. So many thousands of emigrants signed their names that Independence Rock was called the Great Register of the Oregon Trail.

Beyond Independence Rock the trail wound up into the Rocky Mountains. The terrain was fairly gentle, though, because the Oregon Trail crossed the Rockies at a broad, easily traversed pass called South Pass. The approach to the pass was so smooth and gradual that many emigrants did not even realize that they had reached the top of the pass and crossed the highest mountain range on the North American continent.

On the other side of South Pass, several side trails branched off from the main trail. Mormon travelers veered away to the southwest and made for the country around Utah's Great Salt Lake where the Mormon settlements were located. A few travelers bound for California also headed southwest to pick up the Old Spanish Trail. Most travelers, however, continued west on the main Oregon Trail across desert country to the Green River, then northwest to Fort Hall in Idaho, 1,200 miles (1,931 kilometers) from Missouri. Any emigrant who hadn't decided on a destination now had to choose between Oregon and California.

Many of the pioneers climbed Independence Rock to paint or carve their names. A traveler who passed the rock in 1852 found it covered with names written in chalk, paint, and tar. Some of the names dated from 1843, when the first big wagon trains crossed the plains.

Forty miles (64 kilometers) west of Fort Hall, the trail divided. Emigrants bound for California went southwest through the deserts of Nevada, following the Humboldt River until the river vanished into a mass of salty marshes. The travelers then crossed 50 miles (80 kilometers) of water- less, inhospitable desert to the Truckee River. Next they faced the 70-mile (113-kilometer) climb up and over the treacherous passes of the Sierra Nevada range. Here the wagons had to be hauled up the steep slopes with ropes, chains, and pulleys. Then, on the far side of the pass, they had to be lowered in the same slow, painstaking way, or they would break free and crash down into the ravines. Once across the passes, the emigrants snaked their way through forested foothills before descending into California's mild Sacramento Valley.

Emigrants bound for Oregon went northwest along bleak, barren rock ledges in the canyon of the Snake River. Next they faced a grueling climb over the Blue Mountains, which blocked the way into present-day Oregon like a steep wall. Here, too, the wagons had to be hauled up with chains and pulleys and lowered inch by inch down the other side. Sometimes every member of an emigrant train, including the children, clung to ropes to keep a wagon from plunging over a cliff.

Once the Blue Mountains were behind them, emigrants followed the Columbia River west for 200 miles (322 kilo- meters) to a settlement called The Dalles. Here began the final stretch of the journey—and one of the most difficult.

The Dalles was separated from the fertile Willamette Valley by the thickly forested Cascade Mountains. In the early years of emigration, there was no trail over the mountains, and emigrants made the last part of the trip by raft or Indian canoe down the Columbia. Many emigrants lost their possessions—and some lost their lives—in the river's dangerous falls and rapids. In 1846, however, a wagon trail was cleared through the Cascades. It ran west from The Dalles up and over the shoulder of Mt. Hood, then descended to Oregon City in the Willamette Valley.

What made some people choose Oregon and others California? The Oregon branch of the trail was called "the family trail." Families seeking farms and security tended to head for Oregon, while many of the single men who took the westward trail were headed for California. California was said to attract rogues and adventurers, especially after the gold rush of the late 1840s, while Oregon was thought of as more respectable. People in Oregon joked that where the trail split, one branch was marked by a pile of rocks and the other by a sign that read "To Oregon." Emigrants who could read went to Oregon.

For those going to either California or Oregon, the worst part of the journey came at the end, when people and oxen were exhausted and equipment was worn and patched. Usually, the emigrants also felt the pressure of time in the final stages of the journey. Timing was vitally important to a safe crossing. If the emigrants left Missouri too early in the spring, there would not be enough grass on the prairies to

Women and children wait while the men lower a wagon bed, inch by inch, to the bottom of a cliff in the Sierra Nevada. In steep or rocky places, wagons had to be unloaded and taken apart, and every piece had to be lowered on ropes.

feed their livestock. But if they started too late, they risked being trapped by winter snows in the mountains at the end of the trip. The emigrants usually left Missouri in May and hoped to reach Oregon or California by October.

As the travelers toiled across parched deserts or labored for days and weeks to haul their wagons through Utah's canyons while August gave way to September, they looked for ways to shorten the trip. They eagerly listened to hints or rumors of a "cut-off" that might save them as little as 10 or 20 miles (16 or 32 kilometers). Some cut-offs were said to save 100 miles (160 kilometers) or more. To some emigrants, worn out by travel and dreading the first snows of winter, cut-offs seemed like a good idea.

A few of these cut-offs were useful shortcuts that later became established trails in their own right. But others turned out to be traps for the desperate emigrants. Tabitha Brown, the sixty-six-year-old Massachusetts woman who took the Oregon Trail in 1846, told how her party was misled into taking a cut-off by "a rascally fellow." The emigrants hoped that the cut-off would get them to the Willamette Valley ahead of those who had followed the regular route. Instead, they spent months of dreadful suffering on the edge of starvation, fording icy rivers and hauling their wagons up and down the mountains of southern Oregon in bitter cold. They did not reach the settlements of the Willamette Valley until December. The cut-off had cost Tabitha Brown her wagon and everything she possessed except the horse she rode to safety.

Disaster struck the Donner Party, which included Virginia Reed's family, when they took a cut-off on the way to California. They did not know that the "cut-off" was actually *longer* than the normal route. The Donner Party became lost in the trackless, barren lands east of the Sierra Nevadas. By the time they found their way up into the mountains, the passes were blocked by heavy snow and the emigrants could not get through. They were forced to spend the winter camped on the eastern side of the mountains with almost no provisions. Some members of the party ate the flesh of their dead companions to stay alive. When Virginia finally reached the Sacramento Valley the following year, she wrote to a cousin back home in Illinois to tell of the horrors she had survived. She added a piece of advice for anyone who might be thinking of taking the westward trail: "Hurry along," she wrote, "and don't take no cut-offs."

Chapter Four

Wagon
Train Life

When the Great Emigration began in 1843, the first few days on the trail were a mess. As soon as the sun rose, every family scrambled to get under way as quickly as possible, because everyone wanted to be in front. People and oxen in the rear had to breathe the dust that was kicked up by the first wagons; within a matter of hours the faces and clothes of those in the rear were covered with an unpleasant paste of dust and sweat. In the same way, when the end of the day was drawing near people would try to hurry ahead to stake out the best campsites—those closest to the water—for that night. There was little sense of cooperation. Instead, every family looked after its own interests.

Very soon the emigrants realized that things would go more smoothly for everyone if they got organized. Each wagon train elected a leader, who would decide when they would start and stop each day. Sometimes the leader decided

A wagon train winds across the Montana territory. Emigrants soon learned to form orderly lines for each day's travel. Here, flankers with rifles ride on each side of the train to keep the buffalo from stampeding the wagons.

how the wagons would be ordered within the line, and sometimes the emigrants drew lots for their places. Often those who had been in the front one day were moved to the rear the next day. That way everyone had a turn at being in front and no one had to be in the rear all the time. The leader also decided what punishment would be given for fighting or the theft of goods from another's wagon.

Most emigrants walked the westward trail—all 2,200 miles (3,540 kilometers) of it. The emigrant wagons were not passenger wagons; they were crammed full of cargo.

Sometimes a wagon did not even have a driver but was guided by someone who walked with the lead oxen. Only the very elderly, the sick, and mothers with young children rode in the wagons. Some people rode saddle horses; usually the horses were ridden by men, but some women and even a few children rode horseback. In the early stages of the journey west, Virginia Reed galloped alongside her father on her own pony. Later the pony died.

The rest walked. Men, women, and older children trudged along next to their oxen and wagons. Everyone had work to do. The men guided the wagons, keeping the axles well greased and making repairs to broken wheels and harnesses as needed. At river crossings, the men had to drive the reluctant livestock into the water and swim the animals across. This could be dangerous, as an ox or a horse might panic in midstream and start kicking wildly. Men also were responsible for hunting, for defending their party from Indians or wild animals, and for scouting the route ahead.

Women worked just as hard as men. They had to keep an eye on their children—not always an easy task, especially for mothers of large families. Children scampered up and down the line, visiting with friends and seeing what was going on. Women also gathered fuel, cooked and served meals, mended clothing, did laundry whenever they had the time and the water to do so, and unpacked and repacked the wagons. They also made up the family's beds every night. Some emigrants slept in their wagons on blankets spread across the tops of bundles and boxes. A few of the more elaborate wagons had shelves that served as beds. Other people slept in tents that they pitched next to their wagons each night. Many of the men slept in the open, away from the wagons and tents, so that they could take a turn on sentry duty. The older boys considered it a mark of manhood to "sleep rough" in this fashion, wrapped in a cloak beside the embers of a campfire.

Children helped with many of their parents' tasks. Older boys were responsible for minding the family livestock—not only the oxen that pulled the wagons but the beef and milk cattle as well. Older girls were responsible for taking care of their younger brothers and sisters and for helping with the fuel-gathering, cooking, and mending. Girls also milked the family cows. One emigrant girl remembered that each morning she lashed a pail of milk to the side of the wagon; by nightfall the motion of the wagon had churned the milk into butter.

Daily life on the trail followed a routine that Jesse Applegate described in his book about the Great Emigration of 1843. At four in the morning the men who had been on sentry duty during the night fired their rifles. This was the signal for the day to begin. People crawled out of their wagons and tents, shivering in the early-morning chill, and soon the smoke of cookfires began floating skyward. While the women prepared breakfast for everyone, the men rounded up the livestock.

Early morning was a busy time. The travelers knew that before the day's march began at seven o'clock, they had to

Children found little time for idleness in camp. While their mother takes care of the baby who was born along the trail, these youngsters fetch water and tend the evening campfire.

eat breakfast, pack up their kitchen gear and tents, milk their cows, fill their water barrels if they were camped near a river or spring, and harness their oxen. When the signal was sounded, whips cracked, wheels groaned, and the wagon train lumbered into motion.

Generally the wagon train halted for an hour or so in the middle of the day to rest the oxen. People did not cook meals during this break; instead they ate cold lunches that had been prepared at breakfast-time. The basic meal for everyone on the westward trail was the same: bread, bacon, beans, and coffee. When they could, women added variety to their family's meals with pancakes or biscuits, fresh meat, and dried fruits. For the most part, there were few complaints about the dull, boring diet. Most people were glad just to have enough to eat.

Depending upon the terrain, a wagon train could travel anywhere from 5 to 20 miles (8 to 32 kilometers) in a day. The average distance covered was about 12 or 15 miles (19 to 24 kilometers). In the late afternoon, the leader would start looking for a good campsite. The ideal site offered a good source of clean water and grass for the livestock. Often, however, emigrants had to settle for sites that were less than ideal. Each evening the wagons were wheeled into a circle with a large empty space on the inside. If the wagon train was big enough and the livestock herd small enough, the animals were penned inside the corral formed by the circled wagons. Otherwise they were turned loose to graze under the watchful eye of the camp sentries. By eight o'clock the evening meal had been eaten and the sentries were in place. Sometimes people sat and talked around campfires or even had parties, but often they crawled into their beds as soon as it was dark—or even earlier. They knew that they would be awake and hard at work before the sun came up.

Life and death were part of the trip west. One historian has estimated that about one fifth of all the women who made the journey were pregnant for at least part of the trip. Thousands of babies were born on the Oregon Trail. A woman who was expecting a baby had to keep doing her chores right up to the last possible moment, for there was no one else to do them. Women helped one another as much as they could, but most emigrants had their hands full caring for their own families.

Pregnant women worried about when and where they would give birth. Would it be in the middle of a rainstorm? On a steep and dangerous mountain trail? Would it be an easy birth or a difficult one? In those days, it was not uncommon for a woman to die while giving birth. Every pioneer woman who took the westward trail while pregnant feared that she might die in childbirth, leaving her other children motherless in the wilderness.

Most of the diaries and accounts of the trip give few details about the births that took place. A man in Tabitha Brown's party, for example, kept a record of each day's events. One evening he wrote, "This morning Mr. Thompson had a daughter born." He gave no information about the mother's health or the daughter's name, but added that the happy event had kept the wagon train from making any progress that day.

Emigrants' journals also recorded the tragedies of the trail. An account of one day's travel read, "Made an early start from the spring . . . but was stopped by an awful calamity. Mr. Collins's son George, about 6 years old, fell from the wagon and the wheels ran over his head, killing him instantly; the remainder of the day occupied in burying him." Such accidents were sadly common on the Oregon Trail. If a restless child squirmed out of a mother's arms and fell from the wagon, there was nothing anyone could do to stop the oxen quickly. The child was in real danger of being crushed by the wagon wheels. During Martha Gay's trip west, the two-year-old son of the wagonmaster fell out of his wagon and was badly injured by the wheels. He was lucky, though, and survived. Pamelia Fergus's instructions from her husband about the preparations for the trip west included a section underlined in ink, warning her to be careful not to let the children fall out of the wagon.

One young emigrant's story of the westward journey includes a first-hand account of such a fall. Catherine Sager was ten when her family went to Oregon in 1844. Like some other children in her wagon train, she soon grew skilled at leaping out of the moving wagon, although she was warned not to perform this dangerous stunt. One day as she leaped, the hem of her dress caught on an axe handle, and she fell under the rolling wheels. Her left leg was badly crushed before her father could stop the oxen. Catherine survived but was in great pain for weeks as her leg slowly mended.

Catherine Sager's injury was not the only tragedy of her family's crossing. A month or so before Catherine's fall, her mother had given birth to another daughter. Not long afterward, the wagon overturned on a steep bank, nearly killing both mother and baby. Some time after Catherine's fall, when the wagon train was close to Fort Laramie, a herd of buffalo stampeded toward the wagons. Trying to turn the great beasts aside, Catherine's father was trampled. Before Mr. Sager died, he wept to think of the family he was leaving: a wife who was in poor health, a tiny baby, and six other young children, one of whom was crippled. He begged the other emigrants to take care of them. Less than a month after Mr. Sager's death, Mrs. Sager fell ill and died, leaving Catherine and her brothers and sisters orphans. They were taken in by missionaries in southeastern Oregon, but both of Catherine's brothers were killed three years later when Indians attacked the mission.

The children of the westward trail suffered from the usual illnesses of childhood, such as measles and chicken pox. But sometimes they were weakened by exhaustion, a poor diet, lack of water, or long spells of wet, cold weather. Such conditions could turn even a simple cold into a serious medical problem. Adults as well as children fell victim to diseases, especially cholera. The greatest dangers of the westward trail were not hostile Indians or marauding beasts. Disease and accidents killed far more travelers than Indians or animals did. Every wagon train left a few fresh graves along the side of the trail.

The emigrants heaped rocks or branches on top of the graves to keep animals or Indians from opening them. Still, sometimes the graves were disturbed by curious Indians, by animals, or just by the wind. It was not unusual for the emigrants to see human bones—together with broken and weathered wagons and the bleached bones of oxen—along the trail.

Martha Gay knew that death had claimed many emigrants who had taken the westward trail before her. "We often saw human skulls bleached by sun and storms lying scattered around," she said. The young people used to pick up the skulls, read the verses that earlier travelers had written on them, and add a line or two of their own. Martha later re-membered the Oregon Trail as full of heartache:

> We saw many new graves and heard of sickness and sorrow on every hand. Teams fell by the wayside. Pro-visions gave out. Hired hands became tired of the slow

Wayside graves told of suffering and tragedy along the trail. Dis-ease and accidents killed far more emigrants than the Indians did.

gait, lost interest, cruelly deserted their employers and struck out on foot, or took a horse and went forward, in their haste to reach the new country. There was much suffering. Those who had food to spare willingly divided. Fathers and mothers died and left little children to the mercy of strangers. Some families lost all their cattle and had to depend on others as they struggled on, hoping to reach the promised land. Many gave up all hope. The weak and timid fell.

The westward trail was not all gloom and disaster, however. Many of the emigrants, especially the children, had fun during the journey. One youngster who made the crossing at the age of eight later said, "We just had the time of our lives."

Wagon trains offered plenty of opportunity for pranks and mischief. Rebecca Nutting told the story of a woman named Mrs. Barker who was very fussy about her possessions. "She was an extraordinarily neat woman," said Rebecca. "While the rest of us were content just to be comfortable when we camped at night, her tent had to be fixed just so. It was like stepping into a parlor to go into her tent." Once when they came to a river crossing, Mrs. Barker was told that she would have to empty her wagon so that her possessions could be carried across in a small boat. She objected, saying that she didn't want her things to be disturbed. "It was a picnic for the boys to unload Mrs. Barker's wagon and put the things in the boat," Rebecca recalled. "Some would call her attention one way while others picked up a load and ran with it to the boat. When she looked up to see them, another lot would go." Finally the boys carried Mrs. Barker and her stepdaughter to the boat and put them in. Mrs. Barker screamed the whole way, to the great amusement of the boys. "She knew she would be drowned," Rebecca said. "But she wasn't."

The members of Martha Gay's wagon train had a lively social life, especially the younger folks who spent evenings singing and telling stories around the campfire. With no news or entertainment from the outside world, the people of a wagon train had to create their own fun. Those who owned books read aloud to the others. Children played favorite games such as tag, or made up new games. Teenagers flirted, courted, and fell in love. There were weddings on the trail, festive occasions for which women brought out their best remaining scraps of lace and ribbon, men wore their clean shirts, and everyone rummaged in their food boxes for sugar and fruit to make a wedding cake.

Rebecca Nutting told about a wedding that took place on the prairie soon after her wagon train had left the starting point. After the bride and groom had retired to their wagon for some privacy, their friends gave them a chivaree. This was a rowdy frontier tradition in which newlyweds were loudly "serenaded" and teased by friends and neighbors. Rebecca reported that the men and women of the wagon train took hold of the newlyweds' wagon and hauled it half a mile out into the prairie. "Then," she said, "the fun began." People banged cans together, shot rifles into the air, and whooped and shouted until midnight. Then the crowd went

An emigrant entertains his fellow travelers with his fiddle. Sometimes, when the day's work was done, the pioneers gathered around the campfire to sing, tell stories, and celebrate events such as birthdays and weddings.

away, leaving the newlyweds alone until the next morning, when they were greeted with cheers and good wishes.

Frontier girls tended to marry young. If an emigrant girl reached her middle teens, she was pretty certain to receive a marriage proposal on the westward trail or soon after reaching the western settlements, where there were few single women and many lonely bachelors. Rebecca Nutting was married at sixteen, soon after her wagon train reached California. Lucy Henderson, who was eleven when she crossed the Oregon Trail, was married a few years later. "I was fifteen," she wrote, "and in those days the young men wondered why a girl was not married if she was still single when she was sixteen." Martha Gay was very unusual for her time; she did not marry until she was in her thirties.

Wagon train life was often uncomfortable. Emigrants suffered from heat, cold, dust, rain, fatigue, hunger, thirst, illness, fear, and a myriad of other miseries. Yet they were amazingly tough. They clung to hope, picturing the good life ahead. They remained fiercely determined to get themselves and their families safely through to the end of the trail. And at times, as they gathered to greet a newborn baby, hold a party for a newly married bride and groom, or speak a prayer over a trailside grave, they were united in bonds of fellowship that they remembered with gratitude for the rest of their lives.

Chapter Five

Native American Encounters

To the emigrants of the westward trail, the settling of the West was a heroic adventure. Today, however, we have recognized that it was also a shameful part of American history. For the white settlers did not simply build new homes and farms and towns in the western lands; they also killed or drove off those lands' original inhabitants, the Native Americans or Indians. Early in the nineteenth century, Indians from the eastern United States were forced to move into lands west of the Mississippi River. Later in the century, the U.S. government began forcing the western Indians onto reservations.

Not all Americans approved of the way the government treated the Indians. A book called *A Century of Dishonor,* written in 1881 by Helen Hunt Jackson, criticized the government for breaking treaties, allowing the spread of disease, and hurting the native peoples in other ways. But most pioneers saw the Indians as a menace and wanted them to be killed, or at least kept far away from white settlements.

Nearly every account of the westward journey makes some mention of Indians. Often the whites and the Indians clashed violently. Indians did pose a genuine threat to the emigrants—many travelers and settlers in the West were killed in Indian attacks and ambushes. Yet fewer than one tenth of all the wagon trains that rolled westward reported any sort of hostile act by Indians. And most white people failed to understand that when Native Americans *did* attack whites, they did not do so out of sheer brutality; they were fighting to keep control of the lands where they had lived for generations.

Some of the earliest conflicts between the Indians and the emigrants ended in defeat for the whites. Yet the whites kept coming, and in the end their bigger armies and more powerful weapons carried the day. By the 1880s, the last major Indian wars were over, and the Indian resistance had been broken.

Emigrant children always remembered their first glimpse of Indians as one of the most exciting moments of the trip. Martha Gay reported that her wagon train was well into Indian country when the emigrants were startled by "five hundred Indian warriors in paint and feathers, all on horseback and armed with guns, bows and arrows, tomahawks, and scalping knives." The Indians had appeared suddenly, and

As the wagon train waits in the distance, a Native American chieftain warns the wagon master not to cross Indian land. The Indians' desperate struggle to hold onto their vanishing territory led them into conflict with some emigrants.

Martha was frightened, thinking that the wagon train was about to be attacked. The wagon master and Martha's father walked forward to meet the leader of the Indians while Martha and her sister and brothers watched nervously from behind their wagons. Mr. Gay and the wagon master returned with good news. The warriors were merely returning from a battle with another tribe and meant the emigrants no harm. "We were glad to get away alive," Martha said.

Later in the journey, the Gays' wagon train had problems with Indians who tried to steal their horses or livestock at night. This happened often on the westward trail. Some Indians lived by raiding the camps of other Indian tribes, and they saw no difference between this and raiding the wagon trains. When accused of stealing cattle or horses, Indians sometimes pointed to the large livestock herds and said that the emigrants clearly had enough beasts to spare. Often when animals were stolen, the men of the wagon train rode out and recovered them from the Indians without much trouble. Not all such encounters were peaceful, however. Once Indians fired on Martha Gay's wagon train at night. The next morning Martha found two arrows sticking through the canvas cover of the wagon near where she had been sleeping.

Another of Martha's Indian encounters was funny rather than frightening. After the wagon train was far out on the Great Plains, Indians often appeared in the evening, hoping to sell beads and moccasins to the travelers. One day an Indian woman came by with moccasins to sell. Soon she had sold all but one pair. A young emigrant man tried on the last pair but could not get them on his feet. The Indian woman was eager to sell them, however, and she asked if he would let her put them on him. He said no, but the other boys teased him and told him to let her have a try. The woman quickly ran up to him, snatched one of his feet, and put one of the moccasins on it. "Lazy man," she scolded him, laughing. The young man was embarrassed, but he had to buy the moccasins. Everyone had heard him promise to buy them if she could get them on his feet.

Despite such friendly meetings, nearly all emigrants were afraid of the Indians. Women were particularly terrified at the thought that their children might be kidnapped and carried away by Indians. An eight-year-old emigrant boy recalled that he woke up early one morning and rode off ahead of the wagon train on a saddle horse "to explore." Later, when the train was getting ready to start, his mother couldn't find him. She flew into a panic and screamed that he had been stolen by Indians. At once the whole wagon train was in an uproar. One of the men shouted, "There's a horse missing, too!" The men of the wagon train seized their rifles and were about to go to the nearest Indian village to demand the return of the stolen boy and horse when the youngster came trotting back from his adventure, quite unharmed. He was surprised to see the wagon train in such confusion, but no more surprised than his parents were to see him riding calmly into camp. He added that the spanking he received for wandering off alone made him too sore to ride again for nearly a week.

One woman wrote of how she had slept with an axe handle in her hand every night in case the Indians attacked her and her two small sons. On one occasion she stayed up all night because some Indians had built fires off to the side of the wagon train and were singing. She was certain that their song was the dreaded "war-hoop." Nothing happened, though, and in the morning the Indians rode quietly away.

Even when Indians did not attack the emigrants, their behavior made the emigrants nervous because it seemed strange and mysterious. The whites regarded some of the Indians' customs as scandalous or shameful. Emigrant women could not help but notice that the Indian men wore few clothes; girls were ordered to look away when Indian men visited the camps. Sometimes, too, the emigrants were haunted by the feeling that the Indians were watching them from afar, perhaps gloating over their sufferings. When Virginia Reed's party was struggling through the desolate Wasatch Mountains of Utah, they thought they heard Indians laughing at them from the hills—although the sounds they heard could have been the calls of coyotes or night birds.

Despite the occasional attacks, murders, or thefts, the Indians were far more helpful than harmful to the emigrants. One eighteen-year-old emigrant had been warned that "the Indians would kill us before we got to Oregon." Later, though, she reported that the Indians she met along the route were helpful and peaceful. At some river crossings, the Indians operated ferries that carried emigrants and their goods across for small sums. Indians also served as guides for some wagon trains.

Surprisingly, most of the contact between the emigrants and the Indians involved the emigrant women. Indians liked to trade fresh food, buffalo skins, and other goods for items carried by the emigrants, such as calico shirts, wool blankets, and needles. This trade was largely carried out by the women. A man who had traveled the trail when he was

Indians often served the emigrants as guides or ferried them across rivers. These two Indians are helping some emigrants right a wagon that has fallen over.

A trader's camp had both emigrant wagons and Indian tepees. Most of the contact between emigrants and Indians involved trade, and many of the trades were carried out by women.

twelve years old remembered that at almost every camp along the Columbia River his mother would cook pancakes and trade them to Indian women for smoked salmon. Another youngster recalled that he and his brothers had been playing quite happily with some Indian children one evening when his mother found them and cried in alarm, "What are those savages doing to you?" Eventually the boy was able to convince his mother that the young Indians were friendly playmates, not bloodthirsty devils. She ended by cooking a huge batch of biscuits for the Indians to take home to their families.

The words of Amelia Stewart Knight, who took the westward trail in 1853, show how much the emigrants feared the Indians—and how unfounded their fears often proved to be. "I lay awake all night," she wrote. "I expected every minute we would all be killed. However, we all found our scalps on in the morning."

Chapter Six

Journey's End

When the westward-bound wagon trains reached The Dalles, just east of the Cascade Mountains, the emigrants knew that they were getting close to the goal of their journey, the Willamette Valley. But now each family had to make a choice. Should they go by water or by land? By water, they risked a dangerous passage through rough rapids. By land, they faced a hard climb up the slopes of Mt. Hood in the Cascade range. Mt. Hood was the last mountain of the trail, but it was one of the most difficult to cross.

Some of the people in Martha Gay's wagon train decided to go by water. Martha's father and the captain of the train, however, decided not to take a chance on the risky river passage. They would finish the journey on land.

The trail over Mt. Hood was called the Barlow route. It was steep and so narrow that wagons had to travel in single file. When the Gays reached the gate that marked the beginning of the Barlow route, they found many other emigrants waiting to start across. They also met settlers from the Willamette Valley who had come out onto the trail to meet friends and relatives who were supposed to be among the new arrivals. Martha was happy to see these settlers. They made her feel that after months in the wilderness she was at last approaching the homes of civilized people again. As the settlers went from wagon to wagon, asking if anyone had news of the people they were looking for, Mr. Gay and the other emigrants peppered them with questions about the road ahead and the settlements on the other side of the mountains. The settlers greeted the new arrivals warmly but warned that the Barlow route was one of the worst parts of the entire journey. It would take every bit of strength that the travelers and their oxen possessed to get over this last mountain range.

The Gays rested for a few days and then started up the Barlow route. On the first day a storm burst over the discouraged group, who had to walk because their oxen were too weary to pull any extra weight in the wagons. "Old and young were out in the rainstorm," recalled Martha, "footing it up that rugged mountain, over rocks, fallen trees, and through mud and water."

Tempers grew short as some of the people, tired after months of travel and impatient to cover the last few miles of the journey, tried to pass the wagons in front of them. The trail was narrow, however, and lined with thick trees. There was no way for a faster party to pass a slower one, but there was a lot of crowding and confusion. Sometimes an ox would collapse, and then there would be a long delay while another animal was found to take its place. The loud complaints of travelers who wanted to go faster echoed in Martha's ears. A few fistfights broke out.

Still the emigrants inched their way up to the top of the pass. On one especially bad day, the whole long train of wagons traveled only one mile. The next day they reached the summit of the pass, where they were greeted by a blinding snowstorm. The next day they started downhill, but this part of the road was no easier than the uphill stretch. The slope was steep and slippery, and it was all the emigrants could do to keep their wagons from running away and being smashed to bits, or perhaps crushing the people and animals in their path. Mr. Gay tied big logs onto the backs of his wagons to act as brakes. The oxen were removed from their harnesses, and the men lowered the wagons slowly with thick ropes.

Finally the wagons reached the bottom of the long slope. There the exhausted Gays made camp. "All who wished could pass on," said Martha, "and thus we got rid of the brawlers."

They still had some distance to cover before reaching the Willamette Valley, and there remained several big hills to cross. One day they were climbing up "a long tiresome hill," as Martha called it, when someone called out, "See that big stove." There by the side of the road stood a large cookstove that had been abandoned by a weary emigrant. Martha thought that it was sad that someone had hauled that heavy stove all the way across the plains and the mountains, only to leave it behind when the settlements were just a few days away.

After five months on the trail, Martha Gay and her family came down from the last hills into the green and lovely Willamette Valley, a gentle landscape of fields and pastures and woods threaded by a silvery river. There they stayed with family friends who had come west in earlier years. One old neighbor from Missouri invited the Gays to stay with them until they had a house of their own. "There was a large family of them," Martha wrote. "We had played together when we were little children. Father and his old neighbor were so moved by this meeting that they lost their power of speech."

Martha soon saw that there were many differences between the life she had known back in Missouri and life in a pioneer settlement. At first she could barely understand what the children of the other family were saying. Then she realized that they were using Indian words. "They had been accustomed to talking with the Indians so long they had learned their language and used it about as much as they did English," she said. At once Martha asked to learn the Indian language, too, and one of the little girls taught her the words for "no" and "yes."

The children of the other family seemed "wild" to Martha. "They said they never went to school," she wrote. "I asked them if they went to church or Sunday School. They

An 1845 painting shows the goal of many of the emigrants: the valley of the Willamette River in the Oregon Territory. This gentle, fertile landscape was a welcome sight to the weary travelers as they came down the final rugged mountain pass.

shocked me by saying that they didn't want to go." Most of the settlements did have churches and schools within a few years, but even then many children did not attend school. It wasn't easy to carve a farm out of wild land. Families needed to build their houses, barns, pens for livestock, and irrigation ditches. They had to get their first crops sown as quickly as they could, so that they would have something to harvest when the next harvest season came around. Sometimes every member of a family had to work hard for several years just to get a new homestead started. There wasn't always time for school, church, or socializing.

For some emigrants, the end of the westward trail was a bit of a surprise, perhaps even a disappointment. Although they were happy to have finished the long journey, they were sometimes dismayed by the small, primitive settlements they found at journey's end. Most could not build or buy houses immediately. They had to spend their first months in the new territory either living with other people or camping in hastily built shacks or shelters. Some camped in their wagons—and they were already very tired of those wagons. To make matters worse, the emigrants reached the western settlements just as winter was beginning. Some of them had to endure cold, snowbound winters. Others were alarmed by the heavy winter rains. This was especially true of those who went to Oregon, where it rains almost all winter long. Amelia Stewart Knight wrote in 1853, "We may now call ourselves through, they say; and here we are in Oregon making our camp in an ugly bottom, with no home, except our wagons and tent. It is drizzling and the weather looks dark and gloomy." Martha Washburn was thirteen years old when she and her family reached the end of the trail in 1852. Later she wrote, "My most vivid recollection of that first winter in Oregon is of the weeping skies and of Mother and me also weeping."

Those who had wagons and tents in which to camp were the lucky ones. Some people arrived at the end of the trail

This pioneer family outside their cabin in Oregon were fortunate to have such a solid roof over their heads. Some emigrants had to live in their wagons for months after the long trip was over.

with nothing left to call their own. Elderly Tabitha Brown lost everything she possessed when she and some other travelers took a treacherous cut-off through southern Oregon. Tabitha arrived in the Willamette Valley with no money. She found a place to live with a preacher and his wife who needed a housekeeper, but she had no way of bettering herself. Then one day she felt something small and hard in the end of one of the fingers of a glove she had managed to save. She thought the little object was probably a button, but when she took it out she saw that it was a coin. It wasn't very valuable, but it was enough to buy a few needles. Tabitha then traded a few pieces of clothing to some Indian women for buckskin. She made several pairs of buckskin gloves and sold them to some of the settlers. With the money she earned, she bought more sewing materials. Within a few years she had earned enough by sewing to live comfortably, buy some property, and even help found an orphanage that later became Pacific University, one of the oldest colleges on the West Coast.

Martha Gay liked her family's first home in Oregon, near Oregon City. She and her sisters and brothers were able to visit friends nearby and to have some social contact with other families. But after a year or so her father decided to move farther south to a farm in a less-settled area near what is now Eugene, Oregon. Martha wrote that she and others in the family objected to the move because they did not want to live alone out in the middle of nowhere. Mr. Gay insisted, however, and so they moved to Eugene, just as they had followed him to Oregon in the first place.

Another emigrant who wished to live in town rather than in the country was Mary Jones, who went to California with her husband and children in 1847. After they reached one of the California settlements, her husband went out to find a homesite. He came back full of excitement about the wonderful spot he had chosen, insisting that Mary come to look

For Martha Gay and her family, the end of the westward trail was Eugene, Oregon. Back then, Eugene was a tiny, lonely settlement. Eventually such pioneer settlements grew into the many towns and cities that are now strung along the old westward trail.

at it. He took her out into the countryside, stopped the wagon, and waved his hand at the landscape, saying, "Mary, did you ever see anything so beautiful?" But Mary was deeply disappointed. "There was nothing in sight," she wrote, "but nature."

Gradually, though, the emigrants came to feel at home in the western territories. They built houses and farms first, then stores, churches, and schools. Those who lived in isolation acquired neighbors as others moved in nearby. Their scattered rough settlements became communities, then villages and towns. Some of the settlements would one day become large cities: Salt Lake City, Seattle, Portland, and Sacramento. Often those who had traveled across the country together settled near one another, so that friendships that had begun on the trail continued for the rest of the settlers' lives.

Some of those who took the westward trail turned back. Some fell along the way. But most made it to California or the Oregon Territory, although the trip was often longer and harder than they had dreamed it would be. Emigrants who had started the journey strong and healthy were tired and weak when they reached the end of the trail. Many families lost a child, a mother, or a father along the way. Yet most of the emigrants felt that their new homes were worth the suffering they had cost.

The children who had made the long journey west shared an experience unlike any other. They had been part of a mass migration across an entire continent, and they would always remember both the joys and the sorrows of the westward trail. At journey's end, with the trail behind them, they faced another challenge: making lives for themselves on the western frontier.

Bibliography

Alter, Judith. *Growing Up in the Old West.* New York: Franklin Watts, 1989.

Barton, Lois, editor. *One Woman's West: Recollections of the Oregon Trail and Settling the Northwest Country by Martha Gay Masterson, 1838–1916.* Eugene, Oregon: Spencer Butte Press, 1990.

Brown, Dee. *The Gentle Tamers.* New York: Bantam Books, 1976.

Butruille, Susan G. *Women's Voices from the Oregon Trail.* Boise, Idaho: Tamarack Books, 1993.

Faragher, John M. *Women and Men on the Overland Trail.* New Haven, Conn.: Yale University Press, 1979.

Freedman, Russell. *Children of the Wild West.* New York: Clarion Books, 1983.

Holmes, Kenneth L. *Covered Wagon Women.* 11 volumes. Glendale, Cal.: A. H. Clark Co., 1983–93.

Jeffrey, Julie Roy. *Frontier Women.* New York: Hill and Wang, 1979.

Lavender, David S. *Westward Vision: Oregon Trail.* New York: McGraw-Hill, 1963.

Luchetti, Cathy, and Carol Olwell. *Women of the West.* New York: Orion Books, 1982.

McDermott, John. *Travelers of the Western Frontier.* Urbana: University of Illinois Press, 1970.

Place, Marian R. *Westward on the Oregon Trail.* New York: American Heritage Books, 1962.

Schlissel, Lillian. *Women's Diaries of the Westward Journey.* 2nd edition. New York: Schocken Books, 1992.

Stefoff, Rebecca. *Women Pioneers.* New York: Facts On File, 1995.

Stratton, Joanna L. *Pioneer Women: Voices from the Kansas Frontier.* New York: Simon & Schuster, 1981.

Swallow, Joan R. *The Women.* (The Old West Series.) Alexandria, Va.: Time-Life Books, 1978.

Unruh, John. *The Plains Across.* Urbana: University of Illinois Press, 1978.

Wexler, Sanford. *Westward Expansion: An Eyewitness History.* New York: Facts on File, 1991.

Wilson, Nancy Ross. *Westward the Women.* New York: Knopf, 1944. Reissued 1985.

Index